Guess Who's in the Desert

By Charline Profiri

Illustrated by Susan Swan

Rio
Chico
BOOKS FOR CHILDREN

Look closely at
every illustration for a
LIKE THIS ···· **clue** ···· OR THIS
to help you answer
the question.

During the desert's sizzling heat,
guess which critters you might meet.

Who makes X-shaped tracks on the ground
as he chases snakes and lizards around?

It's a...

Who climbs towering, steep canyon walls,
and walks narrow ledges, but rarely falls?
It's a...

BIGHORN SHEEP.

Who strolls along, oh, so slow,
and hides in her shell from friend and foe?

It's a...

DESERT
TORTOISE.

Who has tufted ears and oversized paws?
His tail is bobbed, and he has sharp claws.
It's a...

BOBCAT.

Who nests in a cholla cactus plant,
where *she* can go, but predators can't?
It's a...

CACTUS WREN.

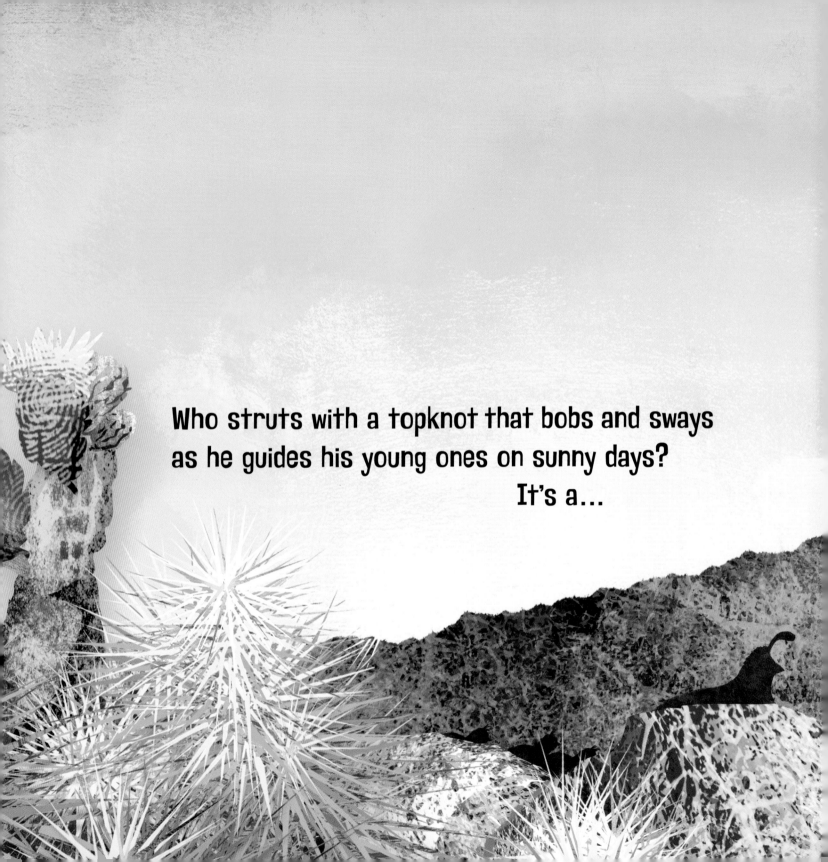

Who struts with a topknot that bobs and sways
as he guides his young ones on sunny days?
It's a...

GAMBEL'S QUAIL.

Who hides beside the dusty trail,
hoping to catch a strutting quail?
It's a...

DIAMONDBACK
RATTLESNAKE.

Who has bristly hair, grunts like a pig,
and uses his lengthy snout to dig?
It's a...

JAVELINA.

Whose eight legs are long and hairy?
Some folks think he's super scary.
It's a...

TARANTULA.

Whose orange and black beady skin
warns, "Stay away or my teeth may sink in!"?
It's a...

GILA MONSTER.

Who can climb trees to search for prey?
Her furry back is silver-gray.

It's a...

GRAY FOX.

Who hoots from her nest in a woodpecker's hole,
on a saguaro as tall as a telephone pole?

It's an...

Whose high-pitched sounds guide her flight
as she hunts nectar throughout the night?
It's a...

LONG-TONGUED BAT.

Who howls a real ghostly tune
beneath the glow of a full moon?
It's a...

COYOTE.

Finally, can you guess
who runs and jumps
most every day,
hops, skips, and yells,
"Hooray! Let's play!"?
It's...

For Teresa and Sara and all who love the desert
— C. P.

For Morgan, Kendall, Roarke, Alex, Zane, and Celese
— S. S.

Text © 2013 by Charline Profiri
Illustrations © 2013 by Susan Swan

Rio Chico, an imprint of Rio Nuevo Publishers®
P. O. Box 5250, Tucson, AZ 85703-0250
(520) 623-9558, www.rionuevo.com

Editorial: Theresa Howell
Book design: David Jenney

Printed in China.

13   12   11   10   9   8   7   6   18   19   20   21   22   23   24   25

Library of Congress Cataloging-in-Publication Data

Profiri, Charline.
 Guess who's in the desert / by Charline Profiri ; illustrated by Susan Swan.
    p. cm.
 ISBN 978-1-933855-79-0 (hardcover : alk. paper)
 1. Desert animals--Juvenile literature. I. Swan, Susan, 1944- ill. II. Title.
 QL116.P76 2013
 591.754—dc23
                        2012019194